Never Fear Anything

Robert Terkla

Never Fear Anything

DEDICATION

To the men and women who have served and to those
who continue. I humbly thank you.

TABLE OF CONTENTS

PREFACE.. 1

I THOUGHT IT WOULD BE DIFFERENT 4

Pucker factor 34

THE BIG GUN 50

SH*TS CREEK.. 82

THE MACHINE 129

AFTERLIFE 148

This is a true story. Although specific events, names,

units and locations have been changed.

PREFACE

Like many conventional forces, they substantially increase the operational capability of Special Operations. Rob's story takes place in 2012.

We are in a desperate fight to meet President Obama's deadline to withdraw in 2014. At the same time, new blood fuels the Zeal of the Taliban as the last of their old guard is wiped from the face of the earth.

When I was approached to write with Rob Terkla, I only knew him from his entertaining videos on YouTube. When I learned a little bit about him, I was eager to help introduce this to the history of the global war on terrorism.

Rob, like me, is an Army Sniper, and we had worked and fought in many of the same places in Afghanistan. Now I had never met Rob in country or back home in the U.S., yet I could relate immediately to his stories. The pressure of perfection is one that is unique to combat operations, and acutely so the role of a sniper. You may be the eyes of a commander, an attack helicopter, or a machine gun team. You may have to asses a ground route from great distances or find the hidden enemy, in his backyard. And when you pull that trigger, you had better be damn sure not to miss.

"Never Fear Anything," is the story of an ordinary man asked to do impossible things.

As you will read this book, and as I have seen firsthand, the war in Afghanistan is now more than

ever a team effort. We are sharing intel, breaking

bread in the same chow hall, and fighting and dying

next to one another. When the bullets are flying, you

are not judged by the unit patch on your shoulder but

your actions.

I THOUGHT IT WOULD BE DIFFERENT

Small rocks and fine Afghanistan dirt pelted the cheeks of my face. Fifteen side-by-side four-wheelers tore through the valley like the Dervish. I rode passenger third vehicle from the lead. I tried my best to keep the fine powder from touching anywhere near the bolt of my sniper rifle. My baby girl, the army's SCAR-H, or Special Operations Forces Combat Assault Rifle. As challenging of a task as it was, I felt worse for the drivers, members of the Naval Special Operations SEAL Team.

As for myself, I wasn't a frogman or special operator. I was just a ground pounding 11B, the

eleven bang-bang. We were what I guess you could call, the extra tool in the toolbox they brought on the battlefield.

We were traveling for a few hours through what I recall to be, some of the most breathtaking scenery I had ever seen. If it weren't for the constant nagging at the forefront of my mind, reminding me this was a war zone, I would vacation here. Fortunately, or unfortunately, that wouldn't be happening anytime soon.

Afghanistan was nothing more than a daily grind. A place I needed to be, a job I needed to complete before getting back home. Although, longing for home combined with the enemy can lull you into complacency. Even "war" can feel routine if you give into it.

Search. Seek. Destroy.

Our life had become that simple. Seek out a contested bit of ground to pick a fight with the bad guys and pray to the war gods, that they wanted a fight. This had become somewhat of the recipe we figured worked best in our area of operation. Today's mission was no different. As always, squads One through Four would carry out the room to room clearing. Weapons squad would help with setting up a perimeter around the village for security. And snipers would provide precision fires when needed. We never knew what to expect or what would happen on one of the search and destroy style missions. But for one reason or another, today had an added electric energy.

I rode shotgun with Chuck. A tall, broad-shouldered, SEAL from Ohio, who had a laid-back California swagger.

"Dude, you ever get that thing in your gut!?" I leaned over and asked Chuck.

"Ha! Yeah, about that MRE, I'm sorry bro." Chuck replied laughing and exposing all the dirt he collected on his teeth.

I knew he knew what I was talking about. Chuck knew that this had nothing to do with an MRE. This was his just his way of keeping me calm and mind in the game. Calm meant cool, cool meant focused and focused meant staying alive.

"Break, break, break…"

The Ground Force Commander, LT. Davis, L.T. for short, scuffed across the radio bringing our 4x4 convoy to a halt. Every cell in my body felt as if they were vibrating in unison, heightening my sense of awareness. Chuck rolled us a little closer to the vehicle in front of us.

I could see a few SEALs from the lead vehicle take a step out and raise their rifles. Pointing them toward a field about fifty yards from us. Through the settling cloud of dirt, I could make out four human silhouettes. My first thought was that we had a case of mistaken identity. Just innocent scarecrows protecting their crops. As I mentioned before, you never know what to expect.

Out of the blue, the scarecrow-like figures uprooted and took off. This wasn't some trickery of a

sleep-deprived mind. The figures became living, breathing humans moving with an intent and purpose.

"Squirters! Four military-aged males (MAM's) moving North West."

A "Squirter," was the name we used for someone fleeing from an area we were interested in searching.

Second squads 4x4's tires spun aggressively, kicking up chunks of gravel in pursuit. Sounding like an awakening beast. Although this wasn't the contact we had been expecting or looking for, it was worth the look and see. Like a police officer stateside would want to pursue someone running from them. Without fail, we found the person running always had something to hide.

Half of the remaining elements pushed out and set up on the surrounding hilltops. Myself, Chuck, and fellow spotter Erick took up a spot overlooking a small village. Five hundred meters to the North.

Three hundred meters to the right of us was a three-man heavy machine gun team.

Eighty yards from the machine gun team, two assaulters and designated marksman. About two hundred meters to the left and rear of them was another two-man sniper over-watch team.

There were still guys around who had my back. I had theirs too, don't get me wrong. Hell, I'd walk up to the gates of hell with them if it were the mission. But honestly, I never saw myself as being a "badass." I just saw myself as a guy with a rifle.

"LT, this is Alpha Three." Radioed the team leader from the pursuing team. The transmission over static-filled radio waves and at times, beginning to fade in and out.

"Go ahead, Alpha Three." Lt. replied.

"We have two MAMs detained. We're going to need to bring a team up here. There's a small village two hundred yards from our location, and I'm sure the last MAM is hiding there. We'll see what these two are trying to hide or if they can point us in the direction of the Taliban." Alpha Three team leader responded.

"Copy that. Sending to your location. Out."

"This may get a little fun here in a bit," Chuck said, adjusting his body armor so that it covered more of his chest.

We all knew that the growing tension in the air was more than the high altitude.

As usual, at first glance, there isn't anything that immediately stands out or seems out of place. It's not like the movies where a sniper looks through his scope and sees a target rich environment. The enemy scurrying around, trying to find the nearest rocket-propelled grenade. In fact, it's almost the exact opposite.

Looking through my 10x scope saw a young lady walking with her child. While no cause for alarm, or a need to call anything over the radio, I felt the need to

want to watch. It was as if my mind wanted to be drawn into wanting to understand what their lives were like.

Wanting to understand what they had to endure in a country where women are viewed as less than man.

"Hey gents, we got lots of movement, Exiting the rear of the village." Chuck's calm demeanor and tone had a sense of urgency I hadn't heard before.

"On it!" I responded while looking towards the south side of the village.

Emerging from a mud and straw hut appeared to be at least twenty women and children.

"I see em'. You want to go ahead and call it up?"
I asked Chuck.

"Roger that. I'll call it up to LT. Rob, you and
Eric maintain eyes on. If you see anything be sure to
call it out. Be sure of your shot, and what's in your
scope, we have friendlies in the area."

Before Chuck could get his hand on his push-to-
talk radio, it looked as if the entire village came to life.
From each hut, emerged dozens upon dozens of
women and children. Young boys and girls trailing
behind what I assumed to be their mothers.

Funny how things can change at unexpected
moments the way they do. One minute you're chasing
what you thought was a scarecrow, to feeling sorry
for the Afghan women and kids.

SSSnnnaaapp! Snap! The sound of reality. It always has the unique ability making us aware of itself when we least expect it. This time, reality announced itself in the form of an AK47 round as it snapped overhead.

Fifty or so women and children now fleeing the sounds of gunfire. Some of the families taking up cover behind small walls. One young lady grabbed her toddler and pressed her deep into her chest.

Here we are in body armor, knee pads, and helmets. Yet she felt assured that the safest place for her child was in a mother's arms. Looking back at it now, I can find a lot of truth in that.

"Contact twelve-o'clock! Five hundred meters!" Eric shouted.

Low crawling, dragging the side of my face against the ground as I moved closer to Chuck's position. My body began functioning almost as if it were under someone else's control. It still amazes me, how the mind can take over in an instance in stressful situations. Your body just shuts off and your training over the years takes over.

"Twelve-o'clock! Moving east!" Chuck shouting over the sound of his rifle as he engaged a target that had initiated the contact. Watching him cracking off rounds at the enemy, the sounds of the bullets snapping around didn't seem to faze him.

Looking through the scope on my SCAR, I could see the plumes of dirt Chuck's bullets were kicking.

"I see him! You're low bro." I yelled over to Chuck, hoping I he would connect and land one of his bullets in the flesh of the enemy.

The only time I had ever looked through my scope at another human being, was to observe. You hear it from the sniper instructors in sniper school all the time. There's a high probability that a sniper never fires a bullet in combat. The numbers being somewhere around ninety-five percent.

The image of the man in the lens of my scope only lasted for a couple seconds before being swallowed up by the terrain. By the time I saw the enemy, they were gone. No time to factor in variables like wind, distance, the speed of the target and so on.

Maybe I needed to be faster? Perhaps I could have at least shot at him? Was I good enough? Maybe Chuck thinks I turned chicken shit. I thought to myself.

"Zulu Five be advised! Three PAX moving at your location. How copy, over." Andy, the SEAL sniper team leader, came over our headsets.

Zulu Five was located on the hill four hundred meters to the front of us. Searching the area for targets, the sniper team to our west spotted three MAMs moving at the base of Zulu Five.

"Zulu Five, how copy, over!" Andy trying to get a hold of them, now transmitting on all radio channels.

"Fuck!" Chuck grunted as he sprinted, hunching over to get a direct line of sight with Zulu Five.

The comms had slight static interference, but nothing that was unreadable. Despite being just a few hundred meters away, everyone could hear us except Zulu Five. Because of their position and the slope of the hill, Zulu Five had no way of seeing the three Taliban.

My line of sight was obscured by tall blades of grass and an oddly shaped rock. Not wanting to move my position and lose my view of the village, I could just make out the base of Zulu Five's hill.

The sense of urgency was creeping towards frantic. Everything that could possibly go wrong was happening in all directions. A routine mission was spiraling further into chaos like a lousy movie. If *"Murphy"* could plan out and conduct a mission of his own, I imagine this is how it would begin. There

were too many moving parts to communicate with each one, to many variables to account for. The reality was each of us was on our own and the only connection we had via our hi-frequency radios, sucked now.

"Damnit, I ain't got shit. Rob, you guys seeing anything at Five's location?" Chuck asked Erick an I.

"Negative. But if they try and flank to their three o'clock, I'll have a visual on them. Erick, keep eyes near Five's location." I replied and giving Erick a new sector of fire.

A last attempt to get the attention of the cut off sniper team, Chuck shouldered his rifle and fired. Put six rounds at the base of Zulu Fives hill. To say that this was SOP, standard operating procedure would be

false, in fact, I'd never seen it. However, it was useful, witty even. Well-trained soldiers can, in fact, orient themselves to the sound of a teammate firing. Despite the chaos of war.

The gravest sin a soldier can commit is killing one of his own. Shooting "at" your own friendly positions was never going to be "OK." However, in the fog of war, all the other rules go out the window. There is a single guiding principle that matters, and that is winning, no matter what. In this game the score is final, there is no overtime, no postseason. Just a single elimination. A sudden-death match between us and violent fanatics.

It was as if some sudden shift in the environment had occurred, ceasing all gunfire for a brief second. The silence was viscerally tangible, like the moment

between lightning and a thunderclap. We got the attention that we were looking for. It just wasn't from the individuals we wanted it from.

Enemy fire had zeroed in on our locations, unlike anything I had experienced before. Chuck dove behind a small mound of dirt covered in sparse bushes, ignoring pinky sized thorns. Erick fired rounds in the direction of the gunfire. Trying his best to slow the deluge of fire the enemy was pouring down on us.

Bullets popped closer in consistent bursts. After a burst of ten to fifteen rounds came brief second or two pauses. The short intervals between each burst kept our bodies glued to the dirt.

By now every hilltop that we occupied erupted in return fire. A pure, controlled bedlam of violence. Zulu Five remained blind to the fact that three men are still close.

"I see em', the base of the hill. One's in the prone to the right of that boulder." Erick shouted.

All the firing must have spooked the three guys at Zulu Fives hill. One of the Taliban fighters raised his ugly, little head. Just enough that I Erick could see him from his sternum to the top of his skull.

You can only get shot at for so long before you figure it may be life changing if you decide to get up and move. Life changing in the fact that you may live or possibly die. Finally getting eyes on the enemy and seeing them for the first time as clear as I did, I felt

relieved. Relief in that I finally had a clear image of what I wanted to shoot. I started low-crawling towards Erick so that we could spot one another if need be. There wasn't much ground that I had to cover to reach him, only a few yards. By the time that it took me to reach him, Erick was already taking the slack out of his trigger and about to fire.

"I got movement! I'm engaging!" Erick said with his voice full of excitement.

A middle-aged male, wearing a sky blue Afghan kurta that drug the ground as he crawled on hands and knees.

"Soon as he gives me center mass I'm dumping him!" Erick voice sounding much calmer than before.

He was lowering his heart rate and breath before the shot.

The man's head thrust back, releasing faint, dark mist into the air behind him. The momentum from his limp body came to a complete halt and his blue Kurta sunk out of view.

Another head rose above the grass and into view, followed by another. You could see it in their body language that they were in a state of shock. The two of them stood up, wobbling, trying to gain a solid footing. More than likely, they were slipping on brain matter. As fast as the two of them stood, they went crumbling back down. The collapse of their bodies followed up by a pair of echoing thuds in rapid succession.

One of the SEAL's on an adjacent hill managed to engage all three targets. To this day, that still remains some of the fastest shooting I've ever seen. Factoring in the distance, taking enemy fire, that's some impressive shooting.

PKM machine guns zeroed in on our hilltop and started raining down lead.

"Shit, shit, shit!" I yelled into the dirt with my face pressing against the ground.

Bullets began impacting the ground in front of my face. Close enough that I could feel vibrations traveling through my skull. Chuck and Erick tucked tighter behind cover. Contorting our bodies like pretzels trying to make ourselves as small as possible.

Screw it! I took my weapon off of safe and started shooting. Sending all my frustration that had been building inside since making contact.

I emptied my entire twenty round magazine, never looking down the scope of my rifle. I wanted to put an end to a dire situation. Each one of my bullets only splashing into an open field behind and around the village. The machine gun team went through a few hundred rounds, never letting off their trigger.

"Make sure we're checking our flanks! These must be the guys you have to fight to get to the boss, huh!" Erick shouted over the gunfire.

As much as he may have been kidding, he was right.

"New target! My twelve o'clock, five hundred meters! Sending." A pause followed Erick's shot. "One EKIA!" shouted. Pointing the barrel of his rifle. "Shit, there's more! Rob, I have eyes on enemy pax with weapons in the open in the village!"

Orienting my scope towards the area Erick was shooting, I saw it. Seven hundred and twenty-six yards away. A man's lifeless body, lying beside a spun out moped.

Erick had taken this guys life and saved the lives of countless others. Having been with Erick on every deployment together, I knew that this had been his first kill. Killing the enemy is something we had discussed in the past, and what we thought it would be like. Taking the life of another human being and talking about it, are on two different spectrums. Of

course, everyone says they could when faced with the opportunity, that's expected with type A's.

Erick didn't cry out in remorse, and I didn't expect him to. As strange as it may sound, there was a part of me that was slightly jealous. I'm by far violent or bloodthirsty by nature, but I wanted to be a part of this, and I was sure of that. We aren't supposed to want those things, but there it was. As real as a stone in my path. I'm not as curious about it as I used to be, though I think about it often. It's the nature of a human being and a mystery that has not been solved by the wisest thinkers in history.

Needing to advance and out of the enemies line of fire, teams on the hilltops began a leapfrog out of the kill-zone. Like the childhood game, this battle drill, woven into their DNA years before combat.

Simple, yet effective. It allows a small team to evade

or advance on the enemy. All the while covering each

other's movements with walls of bullets. Denying the

enemy freedom of movement and keeping their heads

down. Allowing one group to bound a new position,

set up and begin firing. This process would repeat

itself until the enemy was either destroyed or possed

as a threat.

"Sierra up, on me! Bounding up!" Chuck shouted

as loud as he could,

Firing and moving on Taliban positions,

something caught my attention. A few hundred yards

towards the village. It didn't take long to realize that it

was an adult male, carrying something near to his

side.

"Target in the open!" I shouted to the group our small groups began advancing. All my training leading up to this very moment. The enemy had finally allowed me my opportunity to earn my right to be amongst those that I was with.

I pressed my cheek hard against the buttstock of my sniper rifle until it was almost painful. Taking a breath, I relaxed, aimed and focused at the center of my crosshairs like they taught me. The battlefield raged around me. "There you are," I whispered to myself as the figure ran into my view. Starring hard at that crisp, sanitary, thin, black cross inside my scope, I squeezed the trigger.

"One EKIA!" I said aloud.

Chuck looked over at me and gestured with a head nod that he had heard me.

The man I had shot, laid lifelessly. Face first in the dirt. Like someone laid out an industrial-sized trash bag stuffed full with raw meat.

Expanding my lungs as I took in a breath full of air, I wanted to feel that there was a need to realize what I just did. The downpour of emotion that's depicted in war movies after you kill someone for the first time wasn't there. Like the time I thought my mom put an extra chocolate cookie in my lunch for school. And how excited I was because I couldn't wait to eat it. That was until I took a bite and noticed that it was raisin instead.

We continued bounding team after team until all threats had been neutralized in the area. The firefight faded as the Taliban saw a few more of their buddies take their last breath. That's usually how the enemy fights. They come to the cold truth that picking fights with the good guys will get you killed. While we didn't rid the earth of all of them, it sure as hell didn't mean we exfiled with our heads hung low. Our mission was one that would be one in small steps, rather than the large chunks we would enjoy.

PUCKER FACTOR

While not one of the craziest firefights I've ever been in, it is yet, one that continues to haunt me. There's always going to be that one memory that stands out. A memory that you can recall at a moment's notice. No matter where you are or how old you get, you can see it when you close your eyes like it's happening in real-time.

A pair of Solamon sneakers, three-day-old socks, set of my ACU's cut into shorts, sweat-soaked brown t-shirt and my favorite baseball cap. The outfit I

wore, on a sweltering hot afternoon in a small FOB, located southeast of Helmand Province.

For the most part, during the hot, summer fighting seasons, the Taliban attacks in the area would calm down. Between the hours of eleven and two in the afternoon, we were able to move about within the operating base. Of course, there were the occasional gunfights here and there. But they would be over as quick as they started, carried out by some lonesome gunman.

In the military, the term 'down-time,' a time where you are free to do as you please, don't exist. There's always some task at hand or old paperwork that needs filing somewhere. We spent our down-time filling sandbags, building mortar shelters, and cleaning weapons.

With all the work going on inside our base, we always made sure we had someone in one of the watchtowers. We built the tower with almost the same idea as a guard tower at a maximum security prison. Inside, we had enough of an arsenal to hold off a small attack until we could get extra guns in the fight.

One of the older, more experienced snipers in our section operated the tower on this particular day. Sergeant Hank Maxwell or "Gunner." The nickname his team leader gave him when he was a private, fresh out of boot camp.

Gunner was riding out his last deployment before leaving the Army and made sure he kept us well informed. Riding out the last few months of the deployment as safe as possible in a war zone. This

often involved spending a decent amount of time in the tower.

"Hey, Terkla! You check up on your guy lately. I know how you snipers are, always hiding somewhere, huh?" One of the squad guys shouted. Filling and passing sandbags down a human assembly line.

"We snipers are doing just fine. We can handle our own. Besides, we all know how much you really love us when we're watching your six." I replied.

"Woah man, come on, I know it's been a while and all, but I'm a happily married, a real 'family man'!"

As playful as it came across, he did have a point. Not in the fact that all snipers do is lay around or anything. Instead, that I did need to at least pay

Gunner a visit and make sure he wasn't catching a few Zs, not that he would.

I made my way up the wooden steps of the tower, trying not to roll an ankle on spent shell casings.

"That must be you Terkla. Yes, I'm fine, and no I am not sleeping if that's what you want to ask."

"Negative sergeant. I wanted to come up for a bit and see the view, that's all." I replied. Hunching over to duck through the small door frame and coming up with the fastest, and the best excuse that I could.

"Uh, huh. I'm sure you are Terkla. I'm sure you are." Gunner's boots propped up in front of him on the rectangular window seal. Overlooking to the

south were a few, mud Qalat's. Less than one

hundred yards to the west were a row of Afghan pine

trees. Beyond the tree's, lay 1500 meters of open

terrain before fading into the mountains. I would

have a better chance at winning the Powerball, than

one of them getting lucky and hitting us at that range.

Hell that would even be an accomplishment for one

of us.

"No, sergeant, I…"

Pop, snap, snap, snap!

Dirt from the sandbags exploded, filling the

small space with dust. I couldn't have been in the

tower any longer than sixty seconds. Now, it sounded

as if someone was having a fourth of the July

celebration.

One minute, you can go from holding a conversation with someone to wading waist deep into a gunfight.

Gunner started rocking away on one of the M240 machine guns, sweeping from side to side in the tree line.

"Targets in the tree line, one hundred meters! Fuckers must have been sneaking up on us all night!"

One hundred meters!? I mentally exclaimed to myself. That was well within the Taliban's range.

I had my hands on one of the smaller variants of the M240 facing to the North and out towards the edge of the tree line. I grabbed and racked the charging handle backward and forwards on a MK-48 7.62 machine gun. I didn't need much aim at all with

the enemy being so close, all I had to do was look, point and squeeze the trigger.

Gunner was about a third of the way through a two hundred round belt that he kept in the gun at all times.

Sweeping from side to side, watching branches from the trees snap, in half. I couldn't help but wonder why I wasn't seeing the enemy. I couldn't see muzzle flashes, no movement, nothing. All the target indicators snipers use to find targets in the field were non-existent.

Swooooosh! Booom!

Landing between the enemy fire and our tower, a mortar round exploded. Shaking the foundation of the tower.

Swooooosh! Booom! A second mortar round followed only this time it was much closer.

Still squeezing the trigger, the concussion from the blast rocked me onto the heels of my feet. It felt like pressing the 'half speed' button on life. Time and motion moved as if it were attached to the tail end of a snail. Every bullet that fed into the chamber and fired sounded as if I could pick out, grab and count each one. My brain rocked back and forth, bouncing and smashing against its walls of my skull. A bright, white, light sliced through my chest, rattling my organs around like a rock tumbler.

Gunner, target, home, Sargent we got five in, bomb, cover, pain, wife... Random thoughts entered my brain. Each popping and flashing as if I didn't have control over them.

Focusing became a challenge as my vision began to blur. Barely being able to see that a mortar had landed a few feet in front of us.

I could hear Gunner yelling something, but wasn't able to understand what he was saying. I could only make out the word 'walking.' I can only now assume that he was referring to the incoming mortar fire. Anything beyond 1,500 meters, without training, making contact in two shots, is unheard of.

Blood… Wet…My blood. Red…

Looking down at my machine gun and time standing at a standstill, I noticed that I was out of ammo. My firing hand gripping the pistol grip tight. The whites of my knuckles were as white as the bone underneath. The area around me spun into focus like

a drunk coming too. I was standing in a pile of spent

shell casings. Bright, red, paintbrush strokes of liquid

smeared carelessly around the floor and walls.

"Good…Everyone. Rob!" A voice gradually

became clear and time wrapped into a speed I was

comfortable with, but still, off. "Rob! Hey bro are

you okay! Medic! We need a medic in the tower!"

Gunner's voice became distinct as he shouts at the

top of his lungs and looking at me with wide,

concerned eyes.

Silence.

Everything was all a sudden, quiet. No sounds

of gunfire, no explosions, silence.

As the dust settled in our tower, I could see

everyone all lined up and looking over the eight-foot-

tall Hesco walls. Gun barrels still smoking. I can't recall where, when or how they got there. None of that mattered anyway, still doesn't. A comforting thought rose through the fog in my head *"All that mattered was that they were there."*

I was in confusion about why Gunner was screaming for a medic and why he thought I needed a hand down the stairs.

William, our team Doc, came running towards me. I wasn't sure if I had done something wrong, or why he was coming at me at a full sprint. I reached my hand up and out, extending it in front of my body fully expecting to get tackled.

There's that red paint again?

My hand covered in a red, watery substance that ran down my wrist and forearm like the Nile River. My ACU shorts and socks soaked in it.

"Terkla, where are you hit?" Doc came sliding into me, grabbing my bicep and apply a tight grip on it. "Gunner, where did he get hit!? Did you see anything?" By now Doc was patting me down like I was being placed under arrest. Pulling up at the back side of my t-shirt and searching his hand around my upper back. "Dude, I do not see anything, you got to let me know where you are in pain brother."

Pain...

A warm, throbbing sensation sent shockwaves of electric jolts through my hand.

"Fuck that shit hurts! It's my hand. I don't think I'm hit though Doc. Just started bleeding I think." I explained nonsensically.

Doc took a look to ensure that the blood was originating from my hand, and "Well, no shit it's your hand! Hope you don't plan on needing this one for anything else other than shooting, eating and wiping your ass. You have a pretty nasty rip going on with your calluses." Doc exhaled a breath that sounded like he had been holding in for some time. "Damn dude! I thought you were hit! Let's run you over to the med-station and get you patched up, ibuprofen and back to the suck in no time."

We had all been hitting the gym like it owed us money, and for most of us, our calluses couldn't keep up. My death grip on the heavy machine gun had

torn my already suffering palm wide open.

Something Gunner and I would have figured out without Doc. But we just had our eggs scrambled by the blast over-pressure of the Taliban's mortars. It was a bit like being punch drunk, but with high explosives.

As much as this memory lacks a 'fight for our lives' battle, this is none the less, the fight that I revisit every day. When I close my eyes to sleep at night. Before I brush my teeth upon waking. Or, because the time of day, this plays back in my mind. Over and over and over. It was the only time that I genuinely believe that I should have died, shit, I knew I should have died. I tasted it, I felt it, and I stared into its face and then, nothing. No death, no St. Peter and fluffy white clouds.

And in my all honesty, I'm not too sure if I want

to forget what meeting death is like.

THE BIG GUN

It was about four or five at night when Frank and I started our "day." Like every day since we occupied and started building camp Scorpion.

We were in the west tower on sniper overwatch. The tower had become sort of our 'home away from home" tent. We had been in country for six months, and we'd been through hell. A hell of boredom punctuated by spurts of hellish violence.

Now, to give you an idea of the state we were in, at least I was in... We didn't give a fuck. That's not to say I didn't care about doing my job, which was still

my main priority, to do what I trained for and came here to do. I never stopped wanting to be the best sniper I could, and hopefully, if I was lucky, make a difference. I didn't care about myself, home or the shitty chow. The three-day sandstorms, or the fleas in our mattresses. We had been through so much, there wasn't much that you could do to me, or take away from me that mattered. A lot of guys when they have been in country for a long time feel this way. "Home" is an excellent idea, like something you trick yourself into believing is real.

You can only have so many close calls or see so many dead bodies before you stop believing you were meant to go home. No one is intended for anything. You get lucky, or you get chewed up by Russian surplus bullets from some dirt bags AK47. Then,

you're chopped meat. The same as the goat meat we could smell coming from the Afghan's cooking fires. Same as the meat of the young men we killed and left another dead, nameless thing in the desert. It's hard to explain, but it makes you feel sort of invincible at times.

The FOB, Forward Operating Base, we were in was basic. We didn't even have a bunker much less a shooting range.

One of the daily tasks was zeroing our rifle. Our little C.O.P. (Combat Out-Post) was very rudimentary. Not having a shooting range, we would shoot at the corner of an abandoned house that was in the center of our sector. We ranged the building every day, gathering the same distance as the day before. It was the same distance as yesterday, and the

day before. I adjusted my scope, read the wind and fired. The rounds were dead on, just like the time before. I got up from the gun and switched positions so my partner could do the same. Watching through my spotting scope to watch Frank's bullets arc through the air. Their vapor trails bending as the wind pushed the 175gr projectiles. It was like watching a baseball pitch in slow motion. The wake of the supersonic round climbing then fell to its target. Disappeared with a smack into the crumbling adobe wall.

CRACK!

A massive cloud of dust appeared at the edge of my spotting scope as Frank fired another round. Seconds later, the crack of an explosion found its way to us. It was further away than the abandoned house.

But we still felt the last of its energy wave in our chests as washed across the FOB.

I was confused for a moment... That was an odd place for an IED, out there in the middle of nowhere. But the cloud of dirt and debris it made had spread out, not up. IED's are buried pretty much 100% of the time to hide them. When they blow up, they do so upward. Following the path of least resistance, sending a dirt cloud high into the air. This one sort of flattened out and sent its dirt and debris out in a ring. This meant something worse. It had to be mortars or some sort of rocket sent at us on an arcing trajectory like one of our sniper bullets. Lobbed into the air, before falling to the earth to do its destructive work. These were worse because, unlike IED's, you can reload rockets and mortars.

EID's by nature were one and done. They blow up and destroy themselves in the process. Unless the Taliban had buried a second, that's it. That's all there was to it. The danger from that weapon has passed.

"Holy Shit" Erick and I both shouted.

"What do we do Frank?!" I asked of my sniper team leader.

"Nothing we really can do brother. We can't see a weapon, we can't see an enemy. Besides, we're outside of the blast radius, for now anyway. There's nothing we can do about that man." Frank replied. He seemed to calm to me in fact.

Our outpost was in the middle of nowhere, and everything had been quiet since we arrived there.

Naturally, our leadership wanted to see this first bit of action with their own eyes.

Another cloud of dirt and dust appeared. Proliferating, hanging in the air, and then drifting in the wind before diminishing. Its cracking explosion washed over us the instant after we saw it. This one was closer, but still well out of range. We immediately called the sergeant of the guard to let him know we were "under attack." Frank was working the radio. Passing the distance and direction, painting a picture to whoever monitored the radio. There was a problem. By the time we saw and heard the impact, there was already another rocket or mortar hanging in the air. Climbing to its apex then falling god knows where.

Another dirt plume sprang up, closer still, and a split second later, heard and felt it. This one was even close to us than the last. I'm sure the enemy figured out long ago that he had inevitability on his side. It was called 'adjusting fire' or 'Walking in Rounds', meaning each round was more accurate than the last. Sooner or later, most likely sooner, they would make the right change to be on target.

When that time came, we'd be chunks of meat, wasting in the desert. It was an odd attack, especially this distance.

Our FOB leadership was calling via radio to the various coalition forces in our province. Wanting to see if anyone was patrolling nearby. Another dirt cloud appeared. This one even closer. But still far

enough away that there was a delay between the big flat dirt cloud, and the loud boom washing over us.

They could be lobbing these things from behind a hill or dried-up river bed. We would never see them with or without our sniper scopes. Even if we could see them, mortars and rockets had a much greater range than our sniper rifles. They just had to get close, and the high explosive would do the rest.

In quick succession, the Taliban made two more dirt clouds in almost the exact same area.

And then nothing happened. The Taliban clearly had access to devastating weapons but miscalculated the range. Our crowded sniper position emptied out. Yet, we took little comfort that the danger had passed. At best we had received a stay of execution.

The Taliban were fast learners, and this lesson was an easy one to solve. They would be attacked again, and they wouldn't make the same mistake twice.

The rest of our night was uneventful. That didn't change the creeping feeling of dread, scanned the desert-scape.

The Area Commander was supposed to fly in later that evening but deemed it too dangerous. In the Army, we are always taught to lead from the front. It goes to show you where you stand as an enlisted man.

Early the next day, a villager came and told us that the Taliban was planning an attack. He made sure to mention that they were using what they referred to as, "the big gun." After breaking through a bit of a

language barrier, we found out that he was referring to a recoilless rifle. This was a bold move on his part. Given that the Taliban exacts violent retribution on anyone working with Coalition forces.

Being the sniper reconnaissance asset in our AO meant we would get to go after these guys. This was a good thing. It implied my sniper team would be responsible for killing them before they were able to get within range. We needed to get this right. Although there was a factor we wrestled with, and it is the informant's credibility. In other words, this could be a classic bait-and-switch maneuver. The Taliban would go as far as sending a Taliban sympathizer to feed us information. The Taliban could be holding this man's family hostage in exchange for his cooperation. We could be walking

right into their trap. There was really no way of

knowing and doing nothing was not an option either.

My Sergeant First Class was itching to get outside

of the wire. He had multiple combat deployments in

Iraq and Afghanistan, and being stuck in our C.O.P.

was giving him cabin fever. I think he wanted to be a

positive example if leading from the front. Not that

there was any a doubt in our minds that he would be

beside us if we ended up knee deep in spent brass and

grenade pins. He asked that my sniper team stay back

and provide sniper overwatch from the tower. Their

convoy would drive outside the wire to set up

observation posts. All with the hopes of spotting the

guys that were lobbing rounds at us. It was the only

time I ever volunteered to hang back. I could see he

was itching to go and I knew how vital it was to have a good sniper team secure things in the rear.

Watching his convoy leave from the tower.

I was surprised to see him in the second vehicle's turret, manning a MK19 automatic grenade launcher. He could have taken a safer, more comfortable spot in the vehicle as a vehicle commander. It was a compelling counterpoint to our absentee Colonel.

I watched with my spotter from our tower as they made their way to a little knob of a hill. It was designated as their LP/OP (listening-post/observation post). Our information was sketchy at best, but there wasn't much as far as terrain. A small, dirt hill was the dominant terrain feature in the area. Wherever they were planning to attack from,

our LP/OP would be able to see them. Of course, if our observation team was willing to stay out for a while.

That's the majority of what a sniper does. Days of planning, days of waiting after a methodical insertion to your sniper hide site. If you were lucky your target would expose themselves, and you get to take one shot. Maybe two. Then, it's over in the amount of time it takes for you to move your finger and your rifle to settle from recoil.

I sat down and sliced open an MRE and starting 'cooking' some chow for us. Suddenly, I heard the unmistakable 'plunkplunkplunkplunkplunk' of a MK19.

The enemy chose the same bit of high ground to launch their attack from. Sergeant First Class initiated a hasty ambush with the MK19 automatic grenade launcher.

Watching the area and scanning our sector, I could hear our convoy's 50cal and 240 join the fight. The crew served weapons were going cyclic, firing at full speed, drowning out the pops of the rest of the teams M4's.

Things seemed to be working out in our favor.

The vehicle carrying our Sergeant First Class worked its way up to the front. At the small hill meant to be their observation post, he spotted the Taliban war party. A ragtag band of old Toyota trucks and the ubiquitous motos, Afghan

motorcycles. It was our dumb luck that they had chosen the same bit of terrain as us to launch their second attack. Our senior NCO's instincts had been dead on, and now, they were both caught red-handed, and with their pants down. That's when our Sergeant First Class opened upon them with his MK19.

The grenade launching machine gun was absolutely devastating.

The motorcycles took the brunt of the attack, as the rest of the enemies did their best to scatter. They loaded down each of the motos with two fighters and recoilless rifle rounds. They weren't very powerful motorcycles to begin with, but loaded down like they were, the motos didn't have a chance. They foundered in the desert sand clumsily. Our crew-served weapons wasted them and their riders. The

trucks however fared better. One of them managed to escape into the myriad folds of the undulating desert dunes. The other enemy truck was close to its tail, but it wasn't fast enough. 50caliber machine gun rounds punched through the fleeing Toyota's sheet metal. The bullets tore through the sheet metal stirring the Taliban riding in the cab like a bowl of chili.

One of the wounded trucks jumped off its track and coasted into the desert. I watched as it rolled to a stop on its perforated tires. The 240-machine gun and MK19 gave up on the remaining vehicle as it slipped from view. Turning their attention to the disabled Toyota, rattling it with bullets. Anything living in the sheet metal hulk was undoubtedly dead many times over now.

Our recon/sniper patrol wheeled their vehicles into a defense semi-circle. Their heavy machine guns point outward now, ready for a counter attack. The soldiers, who weren't driving or operating the guns in their vehicles, dismounted and began processing the scene. Killing the enemy was good. Learning about their compatriots and capabilities was even better. In pairs, they dragged dead Taliban bodies out of their vehicles. Separating them from their motorcycles. Careful of any booby traps that might be rigged to the vehicles. "They get you coming and going," our NCO's said when we were back in Ft. Bragg, training to decipher pocket litter and pamphlets and other personal items.

Back in the C.O.P. my sniper team leader and I had a few tense moments as the firefight died. The

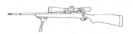

desert can be the quietest place on earth. This seemed

especially so as we waited for someone from our

convoy to radio back and let us know they were all

clear.

Finally, our platoon frequency squelched on my

team leaders' radio. The convoy leader called across

the net to us.

"All clear boys, no casualties. We got the

recoilless rifle team. "MEZ" (short for the base

outside the little town of Mesa Sharif) is spinning up

their Kiowa's to track the remaining vehicle."

They checked the weapons as well for booby

traps. Piling the high explosive rifle rounds and

various hand grenades in a pile. Not long after our

radioman came across the platoon net, we heard a

deafening "CRA-CRACK." I knew this sound. It was several blocks of C-4 detonating the collection of recoilless rifle rounds.

When they got back, we finally got to see the big gun that was causing all this trouble. It was a big win for us to obtain that recoilless rifle out of our AO. The weapon was old and big and powerful. Its range meant the Taliban could attack us with impunity from a distance.

Somewhere in the recoilless rifles journey, it had been separated from its sights. To remedy that, the Taliban had affixed a cheap construction level to the side of it. As the name suggests, the weapon had no recoil. So a little JB weld and the baling wire were all it took to make it serviceable again.

We were all in a feeling proud of ourselves. In our remote area, a weapon like that was hard to come by. Taking it out of the hands of the bad guys would neuter their efforts to drive our small company out of our outpost. The Funny thing about this story, it's sort of a stroke of luck on our part, and a comedy of errors on the Taliban. The Taliban certainly had experience combat proven fighters, like we did. But they also had inexperienced guys. Only a small victory in the grand sweep of Operation Enduring Freedom. Something that would never make the news. But for us, that weapon represented the difference between life and death. It was the difference between sleeping or standing watch the rest of the deployment. For us, it was a huge win that

would change the rest of our time at that little combat

outpost.

Never Fear Anything

SH*TS CREEK

Two guarantees come along with this country during the winter months. It will be uncomfortably cold, and it will be miserable.

Cold, sweaty and I'm contemplating the idea of dropping a droplet of an MRE Tabasco hot sauce in one of my eyelids. Anything to get my blood pumping. I was bundled up in almost every layer of cold weather gear my rucksack could hold. I could still feel the tips of my fingers and toes beginning to numb. There was no reason to keep rubbing my

hands together for warmth. Trying to generate enough heat to make a difference turns into an all-out workout.

The ground was hard as a slab of granite. I never imagined how much I could miss the comfort of a mattress. Or futon for that matter. Throughout my career as an infantryman, I took pride in the fact that I can sleep in, and on, just about anything. I've rested my head on a rock, tucked myself under dead leaves and tree limbs and used Mother Nature as my latrine. The breeze at night cuts like the edge of a butcher's knife. Cutting deep into your bones, sitting there and freezing the marrow inside.

Unlike the high tempo we had in Iraq, Afghanistan was brutally slow. More so like standing

in a long line at Disneyland waiting to get on the ride, everyone's talked about.

To date, I've been in the country just under two weeks now. Despite being attached to a SEAL Team, I hadn't seen any action yet. I could only hear faint sounds of firefights in the distance. Not being able to feel the rush you get when in the heat of battle, these sounds were nothing more than a tease.

Since putting my boots on the ground, we've only rehearsed for the real thing. Sure, it's much needed time with the team and getting accustomed to their fighting tactics. But deep down inside, I felt like I had been through this before. The days start to bleed into one another, and they become too predictable. Sometimes we needed that wrench every

once in a while to get thrown into the norm of things and shake things up a bit.

"Everyone on me! Get up, wake up men. Wipe the frost off your face and stow the letters home to mommy down, it's time to go to work."

Feeling like a vivid dream, was in fact, the reality we'd all been wishing for. The troop commander stood at the center of our FOB. Cupping his hands around a steaming hot canteen cup of MRE coffee couldn't have come at a better time.

"Alright, men, settle in and take a knee. It goes without saying, but I need all ears listening in. All team leads to make sure you take notes and disseminate as required." The L.T. said in a stern tone voice. "As promised, our time to work has come

down the pipe. And as of now, it looks like we'll be headed out before thirteen hundred hours. So be sure if any of you need to stuff your faces, grab it after we're done here."

The taller guys standing in the back nudged in closer. A few of them taking out water-resistant notepads and pins from their cargo pants.

"As I'm sure I shouldn't have to reiterate any more than I need to, but we all need everyone on their P's and Q's. I know it's cold and for the most of us, this is not the operation tempo we're accustomed. We have a few attachments counterparts that haven't been with us on a nine-month train up. Occupying us also will be a small AA (Afghan Army) team. So yeah, let's all watch and police each other."

L.T. pulled a large map from the small of his lower back and unfolds it out in front of him. Pointing to a red circle on the map near the Pakistan border.

"Operation Red Dagger is the name we'll be using for today's operation. Our objective is to secure a small village, suspected to be riddled with IED's. Landmines from the Soviet conflict have been reported in the past, so we'll have EOD and our detection kits with us. We'll be riding a full load so pack smart, nothing you don't need. Our checkpoint is half a kilometer south of the objective, from there we'll ditch the wheels and pick up on foot. We'll also need fighting positions and sniper overwatch set up before the approach. Nothing gets in, nothing gets

out, until we've cleared it. Understood?" L.T. asked, making sure we all understood.

"Roger that." Every team member replied in unison.

L.T. continued his briefing. "Moving along our route and into the village, there is a critical chokepoint. We'll make sure to clear it for any traps Tali may have left behind. Once clear, the ground teams will assist in the clearance and removal of all explosives. Which I'm sure there is plenty of. This area hasn't seen allied forces in some years. I'm sure there won't be any issues. This will be a good chance to get everyone acclimated to the weather and types of terrain we'll be operating in. Everyone here is here because this is what they signed up to do. Any questions?"

To a man, not a single word had to be said aloud. We were understanding of what needed to be done and the tasks at hand.

The time to complain was far behind us, it was finally time to saddle up and get what we all came here to do in the first place. Kill the enemy, regardless of where they may think they've hidden their evil heads and felt safe.

L.T. folded his map and took a small, half step backward. "Alright…Let's get going gentlemen!"

Like a break from a huddle before a championship game, everyone's energy levels at their peak. Everyone heading to their personal spaces in the operating base. Packing up equipment needed for the day's mission, ensuring everything was perfect.

One of the SEALs shouted over to one of the Afghan translators in charge of the AA.

"Aarash! Rash! Bro, get your guys up and ready to go, we brief in thirty minutes!"

Seeing an Afghan with an AK-47 strapped over one shoulder sprinting towards one of us, was strange. Any other day of the week would be a necessary cause to open fire, but not now.

L.T. referred to it earlier in the briefing. There have been some instances in the past with the Afghans fighters that we bring with us on occasion. They were called green on blue attacks.

As with any large organization, you're bound to get a few bad apples. But Aarash wasn't one of those

rotten apples. He and his men were what we'd consider being "legit."

Rash, along with ten of his Afghan fighters, were the guys that shared the same hatred we had towards the enemy. They had a score to settle of their own. The Taliban in the area was notorious in overtaking peaceful villages and towns. They would force the families to fight or use them as something to hide behind when engaging U.S. or allied forces.

As great as it was to finally getting back into my gear and in action, I couldn't allow the excitement to overwhelm me. I've seen it happen to some of the saltiest, combat experienced guys when the energy and morale get high. One second you're fighting boredom, then the next you're heading out into an enemy safe haven. Being the newest guy on the team,

forgetting something was the last thing I needed to happen.

"Terkla. Hey man, you bringing out any subsonic for this mission or not?" Scott, one of the marksmen on the Teams, asked, holding a blue box tip, subsonic 7.62mm sniper ammunition. Scott, one of the spotters on the team, asked while stuffing a spotting scope into the side of his backpack.

"Negative. No need for this one. Those things start getting iffy around three hundred yards or so. From the location we're looking to set up, we'll have our shortest distances at around three hundred and fifty meters." I answered.

The subsonic rounds we had in our arsenal allowed us to take out the enemy or street light

quietly. Traveling slower than the speed of sound, coupled with my suppressor, it was no louder than a sneeze. Although, these rounds also came with some drawbacks. The subsonic rounds often became unreliable, and its accuracy deteriorated at further distances.

Nearing our launch window, the time we ideally would like to strike the enemy, shut-eye was all I needed. Sleep was the only thing that calmed my pre-mission jitters.

Our infil ride to our first checkpoint had been for the most, uneventful. The Afghans that were accompanying us rode in their vehicle of choice, the Hilux pickup truck. A crammed fit for the Afghan commandos. Five occupants in the cab and four at each corner of the bed of the truck. Each man armed

to the teeth with AK-47's and two PKM machine

guns.

The expressions on each of the AA faces were

the exact opposite of what resonated on ours. As they

rode, bouncing side to side grabbing hold of each

other, they remained as calm as could be. As if

nothing was or could ever possibly go wrong. Like

stone, cold killers. I find admiration in that

sometimes.

"Checkpoint One. Checkpoint One, five-

hundred meters. Break…" L.T.'s voice shouted,

ensuring his voice carried over our vehicle engines.

"Heads up boys. Team four, I know you're

tracking the plan on us having EOD up ahead. I don't

want to stay any longer than we need to. I can damn

near smell the Tali's out here" L.T. addressed the

team.

I have to give it to those EOD guys. You have to

have a set of cajones made of American steel the size

of Texas to do what they did.

Sitting on the two sides of us, were two of the

most massive mountains I had seen since being in

theatre. It was like being in the middle of Times

Square Manhattan. Looking in every direction and

feeling engulfed by the skyscrapers. This gave anyone

who controlled that area the upper hand in. Having

thirty or more guys fighting in an area that small,

would turn into a bloodbath in the blink of an eye.

We rolled the last hundred feet silently before

coming to a complete stop. This was a precaution as

to not alert any listening ears. Everyone's eyes glued on the hilltops surrounding our position. Weapons all at the ready, ready to return fire and escape any ambush if need be.

Behind my vehicle I could hear Zeke, the EOD attachment, making a grunting noise under his breath. Like a fighter before a championship bought.

"EOD's moving. I say again, EOD is out and moving to clear."

I could feel my heart beating in my throat. Chuck must have been thinking the same thing.

"Come on now, let's get moving we got to hurry this shit up," Chuck uttered.

During a clearing procedure, things do tend to feel like they take forever to complete. But this isn't the sort of thing you want to rush.

"Zulu One, this is EOD. Everything looks good up here. Let's be sure to follow ducks in a row and keep the speeds down."

"Roger that EOD. Let's move it through carefully gentlemen. Once we clear the chokepoint, we need security and overwatch to break off and set up. Squads two and three, start pushing through. How copy?" Said the Lt.

Each squad's team leaders sounded off over the radios.

"Assault One copies."

"Assault Two copies."

"Assault Three copies."

"Weapons Four copies."

"Snipers copy."

"Attachments all copy."

All of the vehicles started in unison. Zeke, folding up his detection equipment and strapping it to the side of his backpack. Slowly guiding us slowly over his cleared marks.

"Aint this about a bitch!" Chuck spouted.

"Tell me about it. The Army recruiter never said anything about driving over bombs when I signed up," I replied.

Our blocking and security positions were set up along three hilltops. Myself, Chuck and Justin, our comms and security, on one. A gun vehicle mounted with light and heavy machine guns to the left of us. The third hill with the team of Afghan commandos and Hilux, watching our furthest flank.

Stowing some of our extra equipment nearing the summit, we could hear voices over Justin's radio. Growing up his entire life in Boston Massachusetts had a heavy accent.

"Yah huh, you guys hearin' what I'm hearin'. Looks like we got Tali on alert." Chuck cautioned.

"Well, you're the only one who speaks Farsi up here. What the hell are they saying?" Chuck interrupted.

"Wait for a second, this shit takes a minute. It's not like I can just decipher this crap on a dime, Chuck."

"Yeah, whatever you say. Terkla you good dude?" Chuck now, asking me.

Hard to initially make out, Justin's radio intercepted radio chatter. Having taken a few months of Farsi in a language program, Justin was able to make out a some of what was being said. By no means could he hold a conversation, but it was just enough to let us know if someone was sneaking up on us.

Typically, you'd get some interference in the mountains. Most of the time, it was just some old

goat herder talking to each other, like truckers talking

on CB's.

"I'm good, just looking for any movement. I

don't get why these guys would want to fight. It's cold

as a popsicle in a polar bears ass out here!" I replied,

still catching my breath from the walk up the hill.

"Yeah, they got eyes on us alright. I'm relaying

over to Rash and see if we can't get a fix on these

guys. I can make out them saying something about

"seeing the Americans" and "ready the spot." Some

weird shit." Justin advised us on the hill.

"Good copy. I'll call it down to the ground and

give them a heads up the approach may be

compromised." Chuck replied.

While Chuck called down to them, I maintained a watchful eye over them as best as I could. Watching a few of the guys on the assault team through my scope as they move through the village. There was the unsettling feeling, knowing that you're being observed. It made the hairs on the back of my neck stand on end.

Justin kept relaying the ongoing Taliban traffic. Giving us a play by play like he was commentating the Red Sox seep in the 2007 World Series.

"Three males are talking. One of them is directing the entire thing and telling the others, that they need more men to fight the Americans. I also something about, this being a battle that Allah lead.

Rash, believed that they're using binoculars outside the village. Possibly in the wood line near the backside of the objective." Justin informed.

Unbothered by the update.

"Roger that, we'll keep an eye out, I think Haj is bluffing if you ask me. If they hate American's so much, they sure are pretty scared to kick the party off."

Chuck replied.

"I'm not going to say anyone's bluffing this ain't like poker." Justin assessed. "Shit, if you ask me, these booger eaters could be waiting around until nightfall. Watching us watch them. You know?"

The assaulters on the ground had begun to enter and clear each of the buildings. Silently and methodically looking for any signs of enemy activity.

Third squad made entry and cleared one of the larger sized, one story, structures.

"Break. Zulu One, we're in building nineteen in the north-west corridor of the village. I've got eyes on some interesting pieces of equipment in here. There's got to be a few dozen old cell phones, and an unusual amount of ammonium nitrate." Warned Third squads' team leader.

"Roger that Zulu three. Hold in place while I send EOD over to your location. And I know you're tracking, but we're getting some radio chatter from suspected Taliban." L.T. replied.

"Copy Zulu One, we're tracking, still no signs of the enemy. Just kids, women and the elders. We'll lock it down here and continue once EOD arrives, and I'm going to need some of the AA to assist with the children." Third squads Team Leader acknowledged.

L.T. took a long exhale over his microphone before responding. "Same here, no sign. I'll run AA over to assist before we begin wrapping this up."

If you can recall the tragic events of April 1995 in Oklahoma City, then you would understand the concern. Ammonium nitrate, used to fertilize afghan farms, is also, a major ingredient in IEDs.

In the states, there's even a regulation about the purchasing of bulk quantities of the same chemical.

Buying more than twenty-five pounds of chemical, requires that you be screened against the terrorist watch list.

Aarash and his men were a huge force multiplier. Especially when it came to our interactions with the women and children. The commandos allowed us to maintain the mission tempo, without having to use all the guys on the ground. They also were the only ones that truly understood the culture inside and out.

Keeping the children occupied while huddled in a designated 'safe' zone is a priority. As you could imagine, keeping kids occupied for any amount of time is a job of its own.

Aarash tasked a few of his men to grab extra chem-lights and snacks that we had stored back at

near the rally point. Something we learned early on in the war, was that a glow stick and a candy sucker is all you would need to make a kids day.

"Yeah, they definitely have eyes on us guys," Justin said aloud while looking into the distance. "They just said something about guys leaving the mountains. They have to be talking about AA."

"Terkla, how far out you think these guys are?" Chuck asked.

"I'd guess they're well within a grand, easily. Even if we could see them, it's not like we could engage. Those days are long gone and definitely not like the good old days in Iraq. Back when you could actually fire on the enemy and not have to wait to start losing lives."

"Hooyah."

"You're right about that brother. Those days are long gone." Justin and Chuck both replied. It's hard to deny that things have drastically changed.

Behind me in the distance, I could make out the clicking sound of a vehicle grinding through its gears. I took a look over my shoulder to watch Aarash's team approach to rest my eyes off the scope. Sometimes, looking through the scope of a rifle for an extended period of time fatigues your eyes. Not having the traditional sniper, spotter set up, I didn't have the luxury of passing my rifle to someone else.

"AA's hit! IED!" Chuck shouted aloud at the top of his voice. Pressing the push to talk radio button, deep against the side of his neck. "IED!"

Like watching a movie in slow motion. Frame by frame, momentarily pausing in time, burning each picture into my brain. They weren't anywhere near the chokepoint where we expected IED's. The truck had was making its way back towards the village on a path that the villagers must have used every day.

A *thud* smacked hard against my body armor and popping the air cupped inside of my ears.

A plume of black dirt and smoke mushroomed into the sky, engulfing the Hilux. Human body parts flew and spiraled in every direction. Bouncing, skipping and exploding as they bounced and smacked against the hard ground. Mangled metal whizzing through the air, traveling faster than the speed of sound. Each one like a bullet fired from a rifle.

"Copy Sierra. Casualties, I need a casualty count. Over." By the sound and size of the explosion, L.T. knew that the loss of life was certain.

It felt like each of my muscles had frozen over. My eyes stayed glued to the gruesome scene like I was somehow being drawn into it. Like looking through the center of a narrow straw.

"Ahhhhhhhhh!"

A bloodcurdling, painful scream that seemed louder than the explosion itself. One of the AA spewed out of the burning truck. His cammo fatigues charred and hanging off of his body. His exposed flesh melting like hot candle wax.

I've seen dead bodies and a variety of nasty things that comes along with war before, but this was

different. *"What if I just shoot him? Anything to stop the misery."* I thought to myself. At least give him that and put him out of his misery, right?

Two more of our Afghan counterparts poured out of the blown-out windows of the cab.

Concentrated, heavy machine gun fire began erupting in the distance.

"Contact, northeast, six hundred meters, I have multiple PAX in the open."

Suddenly, I felt blindsided by another thud, this time to the side of my helmet, nearly rolling me onto my side. "Get in it, Rob! No time for that shit now, let's rock!"

It was Chuck. He ran over and smacked my helmet with the palm of his hand, bringing me out of the thick fog of war. All of my five senses beginning to come back.

"Justin, relay to ground and let them know that we have a MASCAL!" Chuck shouted, referring to a catastrophic medical event. "Terkla! I need you to get some on targets five hundred yards west of the village."

Rising up onto all fours crawling under bullets flying feet above me, I started setting up my rifle. Going over the distance, feeling the wind, and finally, breathing. Barely visible through the green vegetation, I could make out muzzle flashes. Even with my optics, I was having trouble making out the enemy shouldering the weapon.

I lined up the crosshairs inside my scope the best I could on the bright flashes and started firing. Dirt from my bullets impacting the ground, kicked up short of the range that I needed. I needed to settle down, control my breathing and focus. You forget some of the skills spent practicing for hours every day when it hits the fan.

I've been shot at before, but for the most part, it goes pretty quick. They spray and pray, and you're far enough away amongst a group, that it doesn't feel as personal. This time, I knew it without a shadow of a doubt that each round fired had an intended person behind it.

"You're on it, come up four MILs and check your wind." Chuck shouted out at me, "Zulu One, this is Sierra, we're locking it down up here, but be

advised, we may need to get air up on station. Multiple enemy locations along the ridgeline. Over."

"Copy your last Sierra. I have a MEDEVAC (medical extraction helicopter) and close air support inbound. They'll be on our position in twenty minutes. Track and maintain any and all enemy locations. Zulu, out."

What sets a sniper apart from the regular ground pounder is his versatility. Snipers are just as lethal with a bullet as they are with artillery and bombs.

By the time I could make the adjustments needed on my scope, the enemy would engage us from a different position.

The Taliban fighting positions were well thought.

"Son of a bitch!" Justin shouted.

"Justin, you good over there brother?" Chuck shouted, tucking his head as another volley of bullets snapped near nearby.

"I'm solid. But the damn batteries or something is taking a major dump on us right now!"

We didn't expect that we would be the ones playing translator over the radio for hours.

"Shit!" Chuck grunted through his teeth. "Terkla, I need you to run down to my pack" Another barrage of bullets interrupted. "We're going to be the eyes and ears up here for the ground guys. Justin's locking it down with me. I'll have one of the guys from fourth squad to go with you."

"Roger that!" I replied.

I only moved under cover of Chuck and Justin's suppressing fire. Low crawling and waddling as fast as I could make my way down the hills slope. I could see Chris from Fourth squad, one of the newer guys on the Teams, headed in my direction. His M4 rifle clutched in one hand, the other hand keeping his Kevlar helmet from falling off his head.

"Holy shit bro! What the hell happened at the chokepoint? You see what hit AA? We all thought it was an RPG or something that set this shit off." Chris asked.

"Yeah…" I replied, reaching in Chuck's backpack and retrieved the brick-sized radio battery.

Just as I began jogging my way back to the top of the hill, the helicopters were only seconds out. I tossed over the battery to Justin so he could swap out the dead one and start relaying the enemy targets to air.

"Zulu One, this is Sierra. Choppers inbound and will provide a show of force for the time being. Over." Chuck called over the radio.

With the new rules of engagement, killing the enemy felt like we had to do so with one hand tied behind our backs. A show of force was another way of saying, "flexing our muscles" in the face of the enemy. Just enough to scare them off.

The enemy knew this and it's why they fought the way that they did. You better have all of your

ducks in a little row before pulling the trigger or dropping bombs.

Over in the distance to my three o'clock, was the beautiful site of four, Cobra attack helicopters. Like guardian angels flying feet above us.

Just as quickly as the enemy was in engaging us, they were just as quickly returning and hiding in the holes they came from.

"Sierra, this is Zulu. I need your team to provide cover for the MEDIVAC. AA, EOD and Doc are heading to casualty sight, time now." L.T. ordered over the radio. ."All units be advised, ground will continue to push through while we have air. Standby for a possible overnight stay."

"Copy all Zulu," Justin replied. "Better start setting up some good nighttime real estate guys.

We would be sleeping in the enemies' backyard overnight.

Only the sounds of helicopters now filled the skies. Every once in a while I would catch myself gazing at the crash site. The Hilux was torn in half, separating the cab and flatbed right down the middle.

The teams helping out at the site did the best they could to secure any human remains and sensitive items.

By now, the sun had finally made its path behind the horizon, casting a greyish hue on the landscape. Our air support traded off in pairs. Returning to base

to refuel, then back to provide coverage throughout the night.

The L.T. filled us in as best as he could with details regarding the AA. It turned out that the device used, was some form of the pressure plate. It functioned with minimal use of metallic objects.

By the time AA were on their way back through the chokepoint, the ground had thawed just enough. Allowing the ground to give a little, which in turn detonated the device. There wasn't anything that Zeke could have done to alter the course of history.

We've heard about them before, a few months before deploying. These are the things that you hear about stateside. You never actually expect to come across one. As simple as they by design, nine times

out of ten, they managed to defeat our modernized technology.

The assaulters from first, second and third squad managed to work out a deal with the villagers. They allowed them to use one of the larger structures as a place to sleep.

"Terkla!" Chuck whispered, causing steam from his breath to form around his face. "Dude, I'm freezing my ass off, I know you have to be sucking right now. Layer up and try and grab some rack for a few minutes. I'll grab you when I need you to pull security."

Chuck was right, I was freezing, and the tips of my toes and fingers felt like ice cubes.

I went back to the spot we ditched our gear, about halfway down the side of our hill. We all carried with us a small 'go-bag.' A small bag containing any equipment we would need in cases like this. Each man on the team carries one, holding only bare essentials. One or two pairs of dry socks, compressible sleeping bag, MRE, night vision gear and cold weather pants.

"Not now! No, no, no, no." I pleaded under my breath. The tips of my fingers were now scrapping and scratching the bottom lining with no sign of my sleeping bag.

Giving a once-over to make sure my eyes weren't playing some devious trick on me, I still came up empty-handed.

Although, it didn't take long until both Justin and Chuck realized that I screwed myself out of a warm night's sleep. Seeing a guy in the middle of the night, in almost freezing temperatures, doing flutter kicks I'm sure gave it away. Embarrassing as it was, the both of them got a good laugh out of it.

During the morning hours, about an hour before the sun rises, everyone was on high alert. This is believed to be the most likely time for an enemy attack.

Justin continued monitoring his radio but was only getting white noise. Our air support by now began one by one, returning to base.

"Hey guys, let's start getting our gear packed and locked in tight. Make double and triple checks to be

sure we have one hundred percent on all our sensitive items. I don't want to leave anything behind for the bad guys. And if either of you needs to take a piss or shed some pounds, go ahead and do so now, looks like we'll be heading out soon." Chuck calmly addressing the both of us.

"I am going to take you up on that offer. I don't think I'll be able to hold it the rest of the day, or however long." I replied. MRE's will do that to you. Despite them being a meal ready to eat, most of us here have learned that they or usually ready or refusing to exit.

"Roger that, you're good to go, but don't head out too far. L.T. wants to begin exfil shortly. I'll get to meet up with you again." Chuck answered.

"Heads up! Before you use your wet wipes, warm those bad boys up! Don't ask." Chris whispered as I walked passed him, holding my stomach.

I did my business, and we began making our way back up the hill. Then, that sound again. That snapping sound like the end of a whip cracking the air.

"Get down!" Chris shouted at the top of his lungs, returning fire into a hillside less than five hundred yards to our backs. The both of us dropped to the ground face first. I reached down to unsling the rifle that I had slung across my back and begin engaging the enemy.

"Shit!" I shouted.

There wasn't a rifle to grab hold of. In a rush, I somehow forgot to pick it up. By now, it's safe to say that I have struck the iceberg in the middle of shit's creek.

I was in complete disbelief that I could make such a stupid mistake not once, but twice.

"Stay on me!" Chris shouted, not realizing that I didn't have my weapon in hand.

"As soon as those fifties fire again, we're going to move." He continued.

Without hesitation and on cue, we both haled our butts off. The entire valley shook as the teams above us expended as much firepower as they could.

We made our way to cover. Hugging the sides of one of the 4x4's.

"Two EKIA. Two EKIA." Chris relayed.

Two Taliban fighters must have been watching us the entire time. More than likely, they were spotters sent out to gauge our security.

It was time to shift gears and start loading up the intel gathered. The assaulters and EOD used a few thermite grenades to destroy the cache. As much as I hate it, at the end of an operation like this, regardless of being the new guy on a team, I screwed up. This wasn't my first rodeo, and I knew better. Whatever I needed to do to sort my shit out because my next mistake, could very well cost my life or that of

someone else. And that's something I couldn't bring

myself to live with.

THE MACHINE

Major. Christian Randolph was the name at the header of my paperwork sitting on the officer's desk. It barely had a chance to cool down after leaving the printer tray. Major Christian was the unit's primary health care provider. I've been in and out of his office ever since my injury in SFAS, the Special Forces Assessment and Selection. It became a goal of mine, to be a part of the same group as the guys I was attached to overseas. While the dream of that day ever coming true never came true, at least I can say I gave it a shot.

"This isn't really happening is it doc? I mean, we can't find any other way to go about this? This is it then? I'm done?" I said.

"I've already been selected sir, and I'm just getting my career started. I can't go back out there now, I have a few more years left on my contract. Please, sir, all I'm asking is that we look at other options."

Doc. The title we give the medics in the army. Men and women with the sole purpose to help others.

Why do feel helpless?

It was feeling like my intestines had been ripped out and were lying on his desk. All I needed

was someone to help me pick them up and shove them back in. I could keep going. I'd heal up and keep driving on. What is Sarah going to say? Shit! The guys are going to think I quit or wanted to get out. Sure, the long hours, months away, fights and shit were a little annoying, but that's the army. I couldn't just leave now.

What if something happens to one of the guys?

Everyone's told me how hard it was to get a job when you get out. *This is the first and only time I'd ever been good at something!*

"I understand your concern Sgt. Terkla. But with the given circumstances, this is the only alternative that we have. I wish there was more that I

could do, but this is coming from higher up. Far beyond my pay grade."

"Now, all I'll need is your signature and social." Doc said as he slid my medical discharge across his desk towards me. "You'll also need to head over to your company to receive your records."

Looking at his finger pointing at the highlighted X, marking where I'd sign. It meant giving up my privilege I earned serving my country. One of the greatest feelings I had ever experienced. My purpose in life would all come to an end with the stroke of a pen.

The army was a machine. A well-oiled, megastructure of power. And I functioned as one of the millions of small bolts and screws that held it

together. Like any machine at a large factory, producing a mass quantity of a specific product. Over time, that machine starts putting wear and tear on some of the small screws that help hold it together. The screws integrity begins to fail over time. Eventually, affecting the machines ability to produce the same quality.

As insignificant as that little screw may appear to be in the grand scheme of things, its purpose was needed. Otherwise, it would not have been there in the first place. Instead of taking the screw out and try to polish and patch it up, it's much easier to replace it. The time it would take to fix the small problem, only takes away from the larger scale operations.

"Roger that sir." I replied.

Signing on the dotted line and meant the end of my active military service. That was it.

As much as I wanted to tear those discharge papers and tear them into small pieces and throw it away, I couldn't. I only swallow what little pride and honor I had left, and accept the cards that were given to me.

"Thank you, sir. Am I clear to drive to medical?" I asked.

He knew exactly the pain that I had building inside. I'm sure he had seen it a few thousand times, at least. Guys get hurt all the time in this line of work. Add on the decade-plus war, taking it to the enemy and you'll have yourself the recipe for a

potential injury. This wasn't some wishful to make my situation a palatable one, this was the fact.

"That'll be all Sgt. Terkla. I'm sorry about all of this. I do wish you nothing but success. Medical will have everything there for you and waiting. You'll have to return your issued gear over to CIF (Central Issue Facility) by close of business."

This is such bullshit. I've been to combat, being a civilian isn't anything compared to being shot at. I was a civilian before all of this, there's no difference in who I am. It's only a uniform. Plus I miss being around my wife and seeing family. Ha! Johns is almost back home! He got out six months ago, and he's doing fine. Civilian life can't be that bad.

Driving along the base, there are a few areas where there's nothing but road and pine trees.

Besides old telephone poles lining the side of the road, there wasn't much to see. Perhaps, that's exactly what I needed. A chance to see nothing at all. No war, no explosions, no blood, nothing.

Damn this place reminds me of Afghanistan. I can still smell the trees there. Almost like the ones here. A lot like the mission where we were nearly overrun, and it felt like time was moving at half speed in the tower. I wonder if civilians see them like that too. Do they look at something as simple as a tree and it takes them back to a place in time? Chuck used to say random stuff like that. It could be at the crack of dawn. Right before we knew Haj would attack us like they always did, and he would just say the most random shit. Damn those were some good times. I'll have to keep in touch with the guys once I get back home… But I am home.

I spent the next five hours of my military career driving around the base. Picking up this, dropping off that, signing more paperwork and fighting back the tears.

Despite feeling as if I was fighting a losing battle, the battle that awaited me when I got home, is what I feared the most. My wife, Sarah, knew that my final board decision would come down to today. I didn't want to call her and tell her anything just yet, and I wasn't sure if I knew how to. A new marriage built on the idea that I would have a longer career, giving us some time to grow together. Time to save up some money, have a family of our own and build a house. This is what we had talked about for years now.

I would call from a plywood phone booth on the other side of the globe, two in the morning, Sarah always found a way to pick up. We never talked about anything I saw or went through in Iraq or Afghanistan. We would talk about our future, what was in store for us after I was pinned for promotion.

Sarah would always answer, *"So how was your day today babe? I hope everything went okay and that you and all of your guys are safe."* As small as picking up a phone may seem, it was the world to us whenever someone picked up on the receiving end.

I should stop and grab a six-pack to calm my nerves a bit. Help sort a few things out before I head home. Besides, after a day like today, lord knows I could use a drink.

I had grown accustomed to dealing with stresses in combat and in training. Getting shot at, blown up, a mortar waking me up in the middle of the night was the only place that I had control for once. There's always the chance that I could be killed, but that goes with life. Kill or be killed. Nothing more, nothing less.

Now here I am, sitting in my truck with a 16 oz. can of beer in my lap, jobless, with a family I intended to grow, bills, electricity, water, food…

FUCK!

War was the only place where I felt accepted and appreciated. I had a purpose on the team. Now what? Go home and start looking for the first job? What job? There's no family that I can run to and ask for help, because how badass

is that? From killing bad guys to sleeping on the floor of family members or friends house with my wife.

I sat in the parking lot in front of the base commissary. Cracking can after can, chugging one beer after the other and tossing the empty cans in the back seat. My cell phone in the passenger seat next to me as I stared at it. I played out in my head how the conversation with Sarah would play out.

She's going to hate me. I already know it.

With each can that I chugged, memories that had been plaguing my thoughts began to fade.

Three cans, four cans down.

Who cares anymore? I'm glad that I'm out. At least I can finally travel and enjoy some real free time.

Five cans...Drink.

What the hell did I do to deserve any of this? Screw it, there's always the private military sector, and the pay isn't that bad either. It would definitely pay the bills, that was for sure. But I'm finished with this shit. I'm tired of the long hours, standing in formation...

I took another long sip. The alcoholic beverage no longer held the taste I missed deployed. It didn't have the familiar celebratory aftertaste I experienced after a deployment. No, not this time. This time the taste was different.

Six cans...Sip.

I never intended in coming to this parking lot to get piss drunk. But oh well, here I am. *Better off*

staying here for the night. I shouldn't risk the driving and

adding anymore heartache to the situation.

I was lying to myself. Deep down inside,
never wanting to make it home was the intent to
begin with. The day was already heading well into the
evening and the base traffic this time of day was like
the 405. There's no chance I would have made it
home.

Negative! I'll be fine to drive home. It's only a few

miles away. Hell, I've ridden over the landmines of

Afghanistan and through the streets of Iraq. You.Got.This.

Taking the last gulp, crumbling it into a small
ball and tossing it, I felt like I had stalled enough.
Picking up my phone and dialing Sarah's number felt
like an eternity.

Before I even had a chance to place the phone against my ear, Sarah answered.

"So how was your day today? I hope everything went okay and that you're doing fine." She said. Answering the phone the same as if nothing had changed. Like nothing was wrong.

I froze. Freezing in space with no words able to come out of my mouth. I was confused. This isn't how I planned it.

"Where are you, Rob? Are you okay? Say something Rob, so at least I know you're okay." Sarah voice growing concerned.

The longer I went without answering her. She knew me. She sensed from my hesitation that something was amiss instantly.

"No, I'm not okay alright! I fucking suck at life!" I snapped. For no reason at all, I just yelled at her.

"Robert, what are you talking about? If it's about your medical board, come home and talk about it or I can come to get you."

"Talk about what? How I got kicked to the side of the road like some shit can? Or how about money, can we talk about that?! Can we talk about how I have no idea where we're going pay for anything? So yeah, come home to talk about what?"

I felt like such an asshole talking to her that

way. She didn't deserve it. All these bottled up

emotions I thought I had control over, were finding

themselves a path to the surface. Like an IED that

takes the path of least resistance when it blows up.

We've had issues in the past, just as any relationship

has, but I had never reached this level of anger.

"Rob, listen! I don't care! I just want you to

come home. If this is about your medical stuff, it's

okay! We've been through a hell of a lot worse. *I'm*

not worried about it. You know that. Just tell me

where you are and I'll come to get you. Please, Rob!"

That's when I lost it. It felt like every ounce

of pain and every tear that I had, came pouring out. I

thought that I had all of these feelings under lock and key and I would just forget about them over time.

No lock could contain this. No amount of aggression could shut up the noises that filled my dreams as I slept. There wasn't a whiskey bottle big enough to hold answers to all these questions that I never found answers to.

I'm not sure how life will continue or should continue from this point on. I have no clue what the next week's fight will be. But Sarah, remained there, as she always has. Just like the guys on the team that will walk through hell with you. It's not because they had to, but because they had your back and that's what brothers do.

Finding my place in an uncomfortable world won't be easy, I know. I just hope that I can learn to trust and that I can stay in this fight for as long as I can.

AFTERLIFE

When I set out to put these stories on paper, I never thought about how it would end. That's something many of us never really think about. How it will all end. We know that the end is bound to happen sooner or later. That's one of the guarantees that accompanies life, but e spend little to no time if any, thinking about it. Often, the ending sneaks up on us when we least expect it.

Like my time in the service, it too came to an end much sooner than I had expected. I previous chapters I only touched base on my afterlife. To say I

lived happily ever after, I wouldn't be telling myself the truth.

My truth. Something I tried to hide from to keep the world that I built from collapsing in on itself. Nothing more than some false idea I had planted in my head. I ran from it for so long that I wasn't sure that if I were to see it, I would believe it. The truth is, life wasn't easy. In fact, it was downright miserable for quite some time.

Leaving the military wasn't the hard part. The hard part came when I had time to reflect and think. I never really talked about combat with my friends or family. It's not that I couldn't or didn't want to. I was because I didn't think they would understand.

How could they? How do you tell your wife or children the things that happen in war?

Instead of talking about some of the things that I had bothering me, I tried to suppress them. My go-to remedy was alcohol. At first, I would have a drink to help me go to sleep at night. I would have a few drinks and try and get some sleep. Sleeping became something that felt like a chore. Just something that I had to do, only to wake up to tell myself the same lie. That I was fine. That I was okay. The truth was, was not okay. I lived a life that few will see. It doesn't mak me anymore tougher than anyone, and I don't regret one single moment of my time in the Army. But it didn't make me, me. The person I forgot how to be. The guy before the army, before the deployments.

The truth was, I wasn't fine. I found myself getting angry for no ryhm or reason. The entire

struggle was tiring. I started to feel the toll everything I kept inside was taking on me and my personal life.

The truth was, I needed help. The road that I was on, I knew where it would lead me. I didn't have to hear about it, I could see it. I could attend the funerals and see it for myself.

Veteran suicide, drug and alcohol abuse plagues our generation of war fighters.

The number never lie.

There is no shame in taking care of yourself. You deserve it.

Made in the USA
Lexington, KY
04 October 2018